# Power Wheelchair Safety
## FOR KIDS

By Charisse N. Montgomery, M.A., M.Ed., GPAC • illustrated by Davina Westbrook

FOR THE LITTLE BUG AND THE
BUTTERFLY

**Special thanks to Rose Dues, PT and**

**Richard Montgomery, Ed.D.**

ISBN: 978-0-9861761-5-9

# Power Wheelchair Safety FOR KIDS

How to use this book with children:

- Read the book aloud regularly with the child, siblings, friends and classmates.

- Look up and discuss the meanings of the words *safety*, *careful*, and *aware*.

- Plan safety outings and practice the indoor and outdoor safety skills in this book.

- Talk about the five sense and how to use them to be a better driver.

- Make sure everyone in the family knows, talks about, and practices the safety rules for using a power wheelchair.

- Take this book to the child's therapy sessions and practice the skills with the therapist.

Concepts and words used in this book:

Safety and being careful

The five senses

Paying attention and being alert and aware

Avoiding danger

Backward, forward, left and right

Stop, pause and go

My power wheelchair
helps me to get around.

It's a great way to travel,
but it's also big and
heavy, so I have to be a
careful driver.

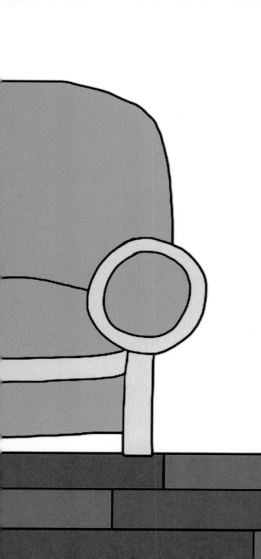

I use my senses to learn what is happening around me.

When I'm driving my power wheelchair, I use my senses to stay safe.

**Safety is important, even before I start driving.**

When I get into and out of my power wheelchair, I make sure the chair is turned off and the brakes are set so I don't fall.

When I turn on my chair,
I check to see that it is set
to the lowest speed.

I look left and right,
up and down,
and even behind me
before I start driving.
I check under my wheels so
I don't roll over anything.

I watch out for people and doors
when I drive down a hallway,
and I stay toward the right side of the hall.

When I drive through a doorway or up an indoor ramp,
I drive in a straight line and I'm careful
not to bump my hands, arms, legs, or feet.
That would hurt!

When I use elevators or automatic doors,
I press the button or switch and move through quickly
before the doors start to close.

I listen for voices and footsteps of people who might be near me before I start driving.

When I drive near people, I watch carefully and keep a safe distance so I don't bump into them.

I have to pay attention because people sometimes stop suddenly.

When I ride in a vehicle with a ramp, I drive up the middle of the ramp slowly and carefully.

When I get onto a bus, I use a lift.
My wheelchair always faces out of the bus,
not into the bus, when I ride the lift.

My chair is parked with the power off and the brakes engaged for the rides up and down the lift.

When I get out of a vehicle in my power wheelchair,
I am really careful. I pause, look and listen
to be sure no cars are nearby,
and I stay away from traffic.

Wheelchairs are made for flat surfaces,
so I avoid stairs or
very bumpy ground.

I watch out for big bumps in the sidewalk
and move slowly to go over or around them,
and I use the curb ramps in my neighborhood.

Safe drivers avoid danger.
I have to pay attention
so I can stay safe.

When something on my power wheelchair feels loose or wobbly, or when I hear my chair make a weird noise, I tell an adult who can check to make sure my chair is safe.

I try not to bump into things or people when I'm driving my wheelchair.

If I do, I tell an adult who can make sure that my chair, my body, and the people around me are all okay.

I steer my power wheelchair carefully, and I make sure my friends don't try to steer or move my chair.

I keep my wheelchair battery charged so I can drive all day long.

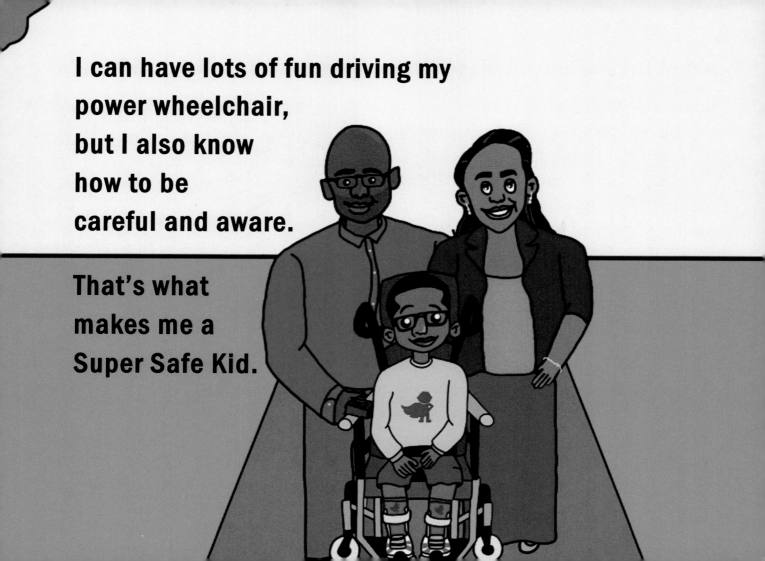

I can have lots of fun driving my power wheelchair, but I also know how to be careful and aware.

That's what makes me a Super Safe Kid.

## About the Author, Charisse N. Montgomery, M.A., M.Ed., GPAC

Charisse Montgomery is the author of the Super Safe Kids book series. She is a writer and editor who lives in Ohio with her husband, Dr. Richard Montgomery, and their son, who was born with fiber-type disproportion myopathy, a rare and debilitating neuromuscular condition. Charisse writes books that engage children, parents, and their families in  improving safety and advocacy in the hospital, the community and the home.

A former educator, Charisse Montgomery has bachelor's and master's degrees in English, along with a master's degree in Educational Psychology, with research focused on informing and empowering parents of medically fragile children. She completed a graduate certificate in Patient Advocacy and serves on the board at University Hospitals Rainbow Babies & Children's Hospital, where she is president of the Patient and Family Partnership

Council. She was awarded the honorable mention for the 2016 Patients' View Impact Award, presented by the Patients' View Institute and The Leapfrog Group. Charisse is also a member of the editorial board for *Pediatrics*, the flagship journal of the American Academy of Pediatrics.

As a special education advocate, Charisse educates and engages teachers, therapists and parents of children with special education needs in the school setting. She has also served on her county's Board of Developmental Disabilities. Her writing can be found in *Complex Child* magazine and *The Mighty*, in addition to a blog series called *Teachable Moments* that she wrote for ProMedica HealthConnect.

## About the Illustrator, Davina Westbrook

Davina Westbrook, raised in Omaha, Nebraska, has been drawing since she was nine years old. Davina is a Scholastic Art and Writing Award Gold Key winner, and won with her piece entitled, "The Parlor." Davina is attending high school and looking forward to higher education with a major in sports nutrition.

For additional resources to stay safe in a power wheelchair, visit our website at supersafekidsbooks.com.

Follow Super Safe Kids books on Twitter and Instagram @supersafekids

Join our Facebook page at Facebook.com/supersafekids

CANCELLED

64941346R00015

Made in the USA
Middletown, DE
30 August 2019